Deanna

She lives in you. She lives in me. She watches over everything we see. In your reflection, she lives.

—Adapted from *The Lion King*

To Kathy

Love,
Marie

Deanna

I MADE A DIFFERENCE

MARIE KONTOS

To order additional copies of this book, contact:
Xlibris
1-888-795-4274
www.Xlibris.com
Orders@Xlibris.com
669896

Contents

Introduction

Death is not the end. I believe most people will be cherished and remembered for how they lived their lives and for the impressions they left behind; Deanna, no doubt, had many. She had a profound impact on people—family, friends, even strangers. Her love for her daughter, Elle, was immeasurable; her energy, limitless; her generosity, unstinting; and her work ethic, intense and competitive. But as hard as she tried, as amazing and beautiful as she was, she couldn't conquer the demons deep within her.

I am thankful for all my memories. They make it possible to transform, to some extent, my deep sadness into moments of joy and even laughter. Elle, I hope that with these words you will discover some of the complexities of your mother's distinctive and remarkable life. This book is for you.

The Beginning

February 11, 1975, was a vital day in America. Gas rationing was becoming a strong possibility even though President Gerald Ford opposed it. Secretary of State Henry Kissinger was looking for flexibility from countries seeking peace in the Middle East, and very significantly, Margaret Thatcher was chosen the first woman to head the British Conservative Party and, subsequently, became the prime minister of England. But most important of all, Deanna Julie Kontos was born at five fifteen in the morning at Daniel Freeman Hospital in Inglewood, California—a perfect little girl scoring 9 on the Apgar scale. She weighed eight pounds one ounce and was twenty-one and a half inches long. I felt so blessed, my second perfect little baby girl.

That day, a nurse came into my room and asked what my baby's name was going to be. She went on to say that my father, a medical doctor on the hospital staff, was complaining at the nurse's station. His complaint focused on the fact that so far, all he had were four granddaughters, and none were named after him. And so I thought of the name *Deanna* since my father and brother were both named Dean. I chose *Julie* for her middle name after one of my sisters.

I was concerned about the reaction of Laine to the arrival of her tiny baby sister, Deanna. I wanted to avoid any possibility of sibling rivalry, so before coming home, Deanna, with her parents' help, went shopping and purchased a big doll as a special gift for Laine. She loved the doll and named her Josephine. Everyone was happy.

By six weeks of age, Deanna was all smiles, even trying to laugh. She was a very good baby; she seldom cried and loved to sleep and eat. By six months, she was sitting; at eight months, crawling; and at one year, walking. Well, actually she was running and rarely slowed down from that age on.

During her first year, Deanna loved splashing in the water, dancing, climbing, and smelling flowers. She was wonderfully affectionate, friendly, and very, very verbal. She especially delighted in playing with Torie, our silky terrier.

By age two, Deanna had become an extremely proficient underwater swimmer, but as in all her activities, she had to be supervised every second because she had no fear and would try anything that came to her mind. By elementary school, she had taught herself how to do front flips and backflips and somersaults. One summer, she was on the diving team for the Newport Beach Tennis Club and received the first-place award for her back dive.

Her favorite preschool books were those about whales, dolphins, dogs, and horses. She yearned to be read to and would carry her books to anyone nearby who might be willing. If they weren't, she had a variety of tactics she'd use to try to change their minds. Sometimes it involved a scream or two or maybe stomping her feet. She was a very persistent little girl.

As a small child with a super abundance of energy and curiosity, she had a few accidents necessitating trips to various emergency rooms. The worst accident occurred when she was four months old. She was sitting in her infant seat on the kitchen counter, watching Laine eat breakfast, when she suddenly fell onto the open door of the dishwasher. She had to have several stitches. Another ER visit resulted from a ride on a merry-go-round horse. Somehow, Deanna hit the horse's head near her eye, and it was off again to the emergency room for stitches. On another adventure, she was climbing from an ottoman onto a chair at her great-grandmother's house, and while at least four people looked on, she fell and hit her head on the television set. That was time number 3 for stitches, and all before the age of three. I was beginning to lose count and becoming concerned about Deanna's safety. As I think back, I wonder if her eyesight might have contributed in part to the problem, because at four years of age, she was diagnosed with farsightedness and had to wear glasses. Unfortunately, she never liked wearing them, and that presented problems at times.

Nursery school was a lot of fun for Deanna. She began at the Presbyterian Church in Pacific Palisades at about age two and a half, attending only two days a week. She was very willing and eager. She wanted to be the first to try any new activity. However, she wasn't all that independent. By the end of the morning and time to be picked up, she would usually be found clutching the fence, watching and waiting for me to take her home. I would arrive, and she would take my hand, introduce me to her friends, and show me her new paintings and the toys she played with. Most important, though, she always wanted me to say hello to her teacher.

Deanna's first five years were filled with many exciting and entertaining times, such as playing with friends, attending birthday parties, going on trips to the snow, visiting a horse ranch, and lots of other fun family activities. At first, there were cousins Michele, Cynthia, Denise, and Stan. Then a baby sister, Georgina, came into Deanna and Laine's life but, sadly, only briefly. Georgina died due to a birth defect when she was barely eleven months old. Ultimately, there were more cousins. Jordan was born when Deanna was five years old, and Cambria and Ben followed. Finally, cousins Chelsea, Spencer, Cameron, Sawyer, and Christian were born. There were lots of cousins, so there was always someone for Deanna and Laine to play with.

Divorce

Nineteen eighty was a painful year. Tom and I had just begun divorce proceedings. At a time when most children Deanna's age are anxiously looking forward to attending kindergarten, Deanna was watching her family crumble. Ten years later, for an English class assignment, she reflected on that time of her life:

> I remember sitting on the couch with my older sister, Laine. My mom plodded into the room where we sat. She looked so sad and lost and lonely. Minutes later, my father briskly entered the room with a black bag, which he placed by the door. As he passed my mother, they gazed at one another for a moment; no words were said, but the looks gave away all they could have said. He then walked over to my sister and me with a placid smile. (I guess he wanted to ease the tension.) He told us he wasn't going to live with us anymore but he would still see us every moment he could. (I could tell he was trying to control any tears so as not to upset us.) He reassured Laine and me that just because he wasn't going to live at home didn't mean that he didn't love us anymore. Presently, my mom said it was getting late and that we must go to sleep. He hugged us so tightly—so, so tightly—and swore this would not break our bond of love. We kissed them both good night and went upstairs. Laine went to her room, but I stopped halfway up the stairs. I looked out the windows and waved good-bye . . . I waved *good-bye* to my father! I couldn't peel myself from the window. It seemed like my face was plastered to it. My eyes watched his car

until all you could see was the black night and the dim streetlamps. My hand could only wave good-bye to the car that was no longer there. My mom then must have caught a glimpse of me, came over, and gently caressed me. She then tucked me into bed.

The divorce of my parents was very, very difficult when I was younger. I felt so ashamed. Now, I accept it quite well. My parents are the best of friends, and I see my dad more than most married parents' kids see their children. He comes down to our house and takes us out, and we talk, have fun— and we still have exciting family times. In a way, I am happy they got a divorce. (I don't mean to sound sinister.) My father is very old-fashioned, and I would have the hardest time trying to abide by his rules. My mom is pretty cool about dating, but my dad would have had a "heart attack" if he knew I had a boyfriend that was older than I am.

Well, I do love both my parents very much, and the divorce—not much that I can do about it now.

Although it appeared that Deanna had a positive outlook on our family circumstance, she never stopped hoping that her father and I would be together again someday.

The Chicken

Deanna scored a major victory in kindergarten. Her class was learning about birds. Deanna, who loved all animals, had begged the teacher to allow her to be the responsible student chosen to care for a fertilized chicken egg over the weekend. The teacher assured her that if she followed all the directions, the chicken egg would be just fine and would not hatch. Deanna was exuberant! So on Friday, she brought home the egg in an incubator. We placed the incubator in our upstairs guest room in a warm, sunny, quiet spot close enough for Deanna to be the perfect "mom" but as far away as possible from Torie, our energetic silky terrier, and Butterscotch, our overly curious cat.

Nevertheless, during dinner on Saturday night, we heard the unmistakable sound of shrill little cheeps emanating from the guest room. Racing upstairs, we saw a little wet head trying to break out of the shell. Our eyes were riveted on the shell before us. Deanna was equally scared and excited. After what seemed an endless amount of time, a puffy little brownish-yellow chick popped out. He was all wet and probably very tired from his ordeal, but he appeared okay. We had no idea what to do next. We made him a soft velvet bed but worried about food and water and questioned if the baby chick should stay in the incubator. Early Sunday morning, we called our veterinarian for instructions, and he was very helpful. Actually, our chick didn't need much. We purchased some chick starter feed and a water container. Chicks are delicate, so it was also very important to keep him away from drafts and to keep the temperature in the incubator at ninety-five degrees.

Deanna dutifully watched over the little chick until Monday morning, when she proudly took him back to school and presented him to her kindergarten class. It was absolutely one of her proudest moments as a five-year-old.

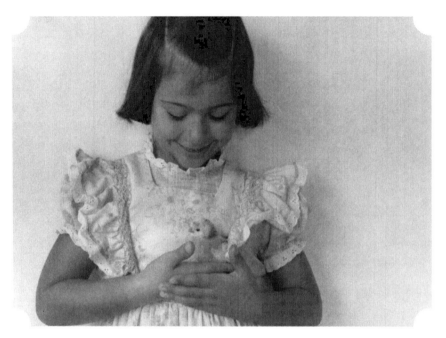
Deanna with her baby chick

First Crush

Barely three years old, Deanna was already passionate about horses. Nasty flies, dirty stalls, and offensive odors were never a concern for this young horsewoman. She would have gone horseback riding every day, all day, if she could have. Being around horses and helping at the stables with brushing, bathing, feeding, or cleaning stalls were her ideal ways to spend time. On several occasions while riding, she was a bit embarrassed because she had to wear her uncle's dented old high school football helmet for safety reasons. Even that didn't squelch her desire to be with horses.

She took horseback-riding lessons, collected numerous toy horses, and studied all about the various breeds. Cousin Denise was also passionate about horses, and she and Deanna played for hours, mostly on the staircase, jumping and talking with their miniature horses.

For Deanna's ninth birthday, the theme was horses and cowgirls. "It was the best party I ever had," she wrote. "Everybody was after me, and I galloped as fast as I could so I wouldn't get spanked."

In preparation for her next birthday, we rummaged through some repugnant horse stables for what seemed like hours, collecting all the discarded horseshoes we could find, many with nails still attached in them, broken and rusty. Finally, we had gathered about twenty horseshoes and were ready for the next step. The shoes needed hours of preparation for our unique and creative art project. This required cleaning and scrubbing the shoes with industrial-strength brushes. It was worth all the effort. On the day of the party, the guests had a great time painting and decorating their own real good-luck horseshoe. They made beaded leather necklaces, and they ate a cake that was decorated like a magnificent stallion. Games and races followed, with all the kids galloping, trotting, or jumping around the yard.

On one of our family vacations, we went to the Madonna Inn in Northern California. As soon as we arrived, Deanna spotted several horses in a corral, jumped out of the van, climbed over a couple of fences, and raced over to pet all of them. Nothing was going to detract her as she ignored our loud screams to stop and wait. She was oblivious to any thought of potential danger, much less the strong smell of manure.

But by the sixth grade, Deanna's love of horses was replaced by one special dog, Sabra.

Sabra

Deanna was eleven when she was accepted by the 4-H club to raise a puppy for Guide Dogs for the Blind in San Rafael, California. There, German shepherds, Labrador retrievers, and golden retrievers are carefully bred and trained to act as guide dogs for people who are visually handicapped. Adults and children can apply to raise and socialize their puppies for approximately one year. Then the puppies are returned for the actual training in assisting the blind.

After a few months' wait, the big day finally arrived. Deanna's puppy would be arriving by plane to Orange County. We were to meet her puppy at the Orange County Fairgrounds along with other puppy raisers and their new puppies. The pup had been given the name *Sabra* while in San Rafael, and Deanna thought she was absolutely the cutest, sweetest yellow Labrador ever. It was love at first sight.

As the two were getting acquainted, Sabra saw a cat and went over for a closer look. The cat was frightened and scratched Sabra's eye—not exactly a great start for a future seeing-eye dog. Luckily, a veterinarian was nearby and rendered first aid, and fortunately, Sabra's eye was not injured.

Deanna was assigned the task of teaching Sabra basic obedience skills and exposing her to all kinds of people, lots of dogs, and places like restaurants, grocery stores, schools, and even airports. They also had to attend training meetings about once a month. Deanna was only in seventh grade, but she knew the importance of her job and was devoted to it and to Sabra.

One day, the happy twosome was on one of their walks, when two large dogs, off leash, came running up to Sabra. One growled and tried to bite Sabra. Without regard to her safety, Deanna grabbed Sabra and held her above her head. The dogs were jumping and trying to reach

Sabra. Luckily, the dog's owner heard all the commotion and got her dogs. Sabra wasn't harmed, but Deanna had scratches and cuts on her upper arms and forearms.

At the next meeting, Deanna was given an award for bravery, having saved her puppy from possible serious injury.

Deanna and Sabra were completely bonded. Sabra wore a harness indicating she was "a guide dog in training" and therefore was allowed to go places most dogs were not allowed. Deanna proudly took Sabra everywhere she could imagine, and they attended all the puppy-training meetings. However, I think both of them mostly loved cuddling and even swimming together. They participated in the Riverside Field Days, winning second place. Sabra also won third place in a Halloween contest. I can still picture the costume Deanna had put on her.

Deanna was very conflicted, very sad, when the time to give Sabra up came. Although she had raised Sabra for the purpose of eventually helping the blind, she loved her so much that the separation was extremely difficult. The year had passed quickly, and Sabra had to return to San Rafael for her actual guide-dog training. Deanna followed her progress almost daily. Sabra was perfect in temperament and bone structure, and so the guide-dog instructors planned to have her become a breeder dog. But first, Sabra would have to complete the initial guide-dog training like all the other puppies. However, one day, while being driven around in the guide-dog puppy truck, Sabra chewed the carpet. Nothing new; she always loved to chew, especially shoes and slippers. As a result, the instructors thought she might have a little too much chewing instinct and decided she was best suited to be a regular guide dog. But during Sabra's last few days of training, with only about a week left before she was scheduled to meet her permanent partner, a motorcycle speeding by came too close to her. Sabra was scared and bolted into a San Francisco street. So Sabra's stay in San Rafael was extended for a month while trainers tried over and over to get her used to the loud noise of motorcycles. Nothing worked.

Although Guide Dogs for the Blind was disappointed, it was great news for Deanna. Sabra came back to her, and what a happy day it was! I remember picking Sabra up at the airport, her tail wagging so hard that when she saw Deanna, she practically knocked the whole kennel over.

Sabra and Deanna

The True Story of the Broken Arm

When Deanna was about five, she broke her arm in one of the most ridiculous ways imaginable. It had been a routine afternoon. Laine and Deanna were at the local neighborhood playground. There was a swing set with two big-girl swings and a very large, unusually shaped Indian head mounted at the top. Although the Indian head was merely decorative, the older children regularly climbed up the swing set, got to the top, and jumped from it, usually landing safely on the sandy ground. It appealed to the girls and especially to Deanna. So on this day, Deanna decided she would climb up the swing set and jump from the Indian head on top. Laine warned her not to do it, but Deanna insisted she would be fine because . . . well, because "I can fly!"

"No, you can't fly," shouted Laine.

"Oh, I can fly," yelled Deanna. "I can. Watch me."

And so, flapping her arms, she leaped off the top of the swing. No, she couldn't fly. She landed hard and directly on her arm. She didn't cry or scream, but they both immediately knew that something was very wrong.

Deanna was worried about still another trip to the emergency room, and Laine felt responsible. She was, after all, the older sister. Deanna came up with an idea for a cover-up since both she and Laine were feeling guilty and did not want to get in trouble. They wouldn't mention the fall, and Deanna would play "Indian chief" so she could keep her arms folded across her chest. That's what she did. The next day, when their dad came over to take all of us to dinner, he told Deanna to put on a sweater. She said no, that she was playing Indian chief. When her dad insisted and took her arm to put into her sweater, Deanna screamed, and their scheme was exposed. Dinner was delayed. It was off to the emergency room, where she was X-rayed then given her first cast.

The funniest part of the whole experience was that after the cast was put on, Deanna didn't slow down. She still behaved like her arm was just fine and would run, play, and swim as though the cast were nonexistent. At the pool, Deanna would insist she just wanted to sit on the side and dangle her feet in the water. I said okay, as long as she promised she'd keep her cast dry. Two seconds later, however, she would somehow manage to fall in. Her exuberance resulted in several follow-up trips to the doctor. Besides being soggy, there were times when the cast was bent, dirty, unraveling, and marked up with all kinds of messages from her friends. Oh, and rather smelly too. The doctor was irritated each time he saw her, because he had to put on one cast after another.

The sisters teased each other for years as to what actually led Deanna to jump from the Indian head. Regardless of the answer, as adventurous, daring, and undaunted as Deanna's spirit was, she probably, in her heart, believed that she could fly.

Ridgecrest Cousins

Ridgecrest, formerly called Crumville, was incorporated as a city in 1963. It is located in the Indian Wells Valley in Northeastern Kern County, California, adjacent to the Naval Air Weapons Station China Lake. The population is approximately twenty-five thousand. Four mountain ranges surround this unique high-desert community.

Ridgecrest was home to Laine and Deanna's first generation of cousins: Michele, Cynthia, Denise, and Stanley. They lived there mostly during their elementary school and teenage years. Their family moved to Ridgecrest because Laine and Deanna's aunt and uncle wanted their children to grow up in a small town near the mountains, away from the pollution and congestion of the city. Uncle Denny was starting his medical practice as a cardiologist, and Ridgecrest seemed like the perfect place for their family. And it was!

Nicknames were a priority. Michele was Mitch, Cynthia was Squid, Stanley was shortened to Stan, Laine was Liz or Lazer, and Deanna was Driz or Banana. Denise was Nanner, and Deanna and Denise together were the Double Ds or Double Disasters. In retrospect, Cynthia recalled, "I can still hear Deanna's usual excited 'Squid!' every time we met one another, which just automatically made me feel good no matter what kind of day I was having."

Denise and Deanna liked to do things a little differently, sometimes taking risks. Once, they were exploring in the area close to Deanna's house, and they found themselves at the top of a cliff. It was about thirty feet high, with lots of brush, rocks, and gullies. Denise remembered that Deanna wanted to plunge straight down, and so they did. Both of them were pretty seriously scratched, but they had fun.

Countless weekends were spent in Ridgecrest, Lake Arrowhead, Palm Desert, Los Angeles, with special trips to Hearst Castle, Arizona, Yosemite, Mammoth Mountain, and San Francisco. Aunt Gaby and Uncle Denny had a large van, and Deanna loved to sing and entertain everyone during the long rides. Her favorite songs were "Brown Eyed Girl" and "Blue Moon." She would drag out the words "Bluuuuuuuuue moooon, you saw me standing aloooooone!" "I can hear it like it was yesterday, and I'm laughing in my chair right now remembering this," wrote Cynthia. Denise recalled a song by Pink Floyd that Deanna liked, especially the lyrics "We don't need no education, we don't need no forced control." Denise always thought Deanna was very intelligent, a free spirit who liked learning about life through people. She did well in school when she put her mind to it but often chose not to experience life in moderation. As a result, she sometimes found herself in trouble.

When visiting Ridgecrest, Laine and Deanna always looked forward to spending lots of time at the Pinafore, a children's clothing store owned by their Aunt Gabriela. There they tried on the latest fashions and usually ended up buying at least one stylish outfit.

St. Sophia Greek Camp in Lake Arrowhead provided the cousins with weeks of summer fun together. One year, Deanna had a crush on a lifeguard named Pete. Cynthia had a little crush on his brother. They spent the summer scheming how they could all get together outside the camp. In the end, they never did. Cynthia recalled that Deanna's soft and sensitive heart kept all those close to her once she let them in, and subsequently, she talked about Pete for years. It was just sweet childhood adoration. Deanna sure knew how to spot the nicest guy in the crowd. Pete was a genuinely kind person, and so was his brother Bill, who later became a priest.

Year-round, many weekends were spent at the Lake Arrowhead cabin. Favorite activities included horseback riding, swinging on a tire hung between two towering trees, swimming in the lake, playing various games on the hammocks, raking pine needles, and taking long hikes. On those hikes, Deanna would always make friends with the neighborhood dogs, most of whom were allowed the freedom to explore the area. Her favorite might have been the special dog with two different-colored eyes. Deanna had a way with animals, and this dog and several others would follow everyone home, led by Deanna. Then they would hang around the cabin, craving attention and, of course, food.

Usually, in the cabin, the kids slept upstairs; the grown-ups, downstairs. Each upstairs bed had a name. One was the "wet bed," also known as the "pee bed," and one was the "snoring bed." No one wanted the bed in the corner because that one was scary. The kids would all talk and giggle while the grown-ups were downstairs, often playing Scrabble. Every once in a while, it would get too loud, and they'd shout upstairs for the kids to quiet down. Presumably, the Double Ds would be blamed for the noise. According to Cynthia, the Double Ds would usually figure out a way of adding a little mischievous activity to the group, all in good fun.

As the cousins grew up, they saw each other less frequently. Colleges were attended all over the country. There were travels to Europe and Asia. Cynthia and Michele lived in different countries, and the older cousins were marrying and starting families of their own. Still, everyone managed to get together, a trip here and there, and especially at Christmas and other holidays.

Lost Love

When Deanna was in the eighth grade, she enjoyed the companionship of a first boyfriend, Josh. He was considerate, attentive, and kind, and he walked Deanna home from school most every day.

In her autobiography, written while in tenth grade, Deanna described him as being "tall with brown hair, green eyes, and a body of steel. He was very smart and, unlike other boys, was very in tune with his feelings. . . . We dated about two weeks, and then he kissed me. How romantic! He was my bridge when troubled waters arose."

Josh was experiencing severe family issues while living with his father. He complained his father was never home, which upset him quite a bit. The courtship of Deanna and Josh was rather brief. They had broken up a few times. The last time they talked, they ended up arguing, and he said, "Well, see ya in another lifetime." Three days later, Josh committed suicide.

Understandably, Deanna was extremely upset. She wrote, for an English assignment, "I still can't believe he is gone. We were born on the same day! I miss him so much. A lot of times, I thought if I died I could be with him, but what if there is no heaven? I would be lost. My senses yearn for his touch, my mind misses his kind words, my heart misses its true love, its first love, and its lost love."

Psychologists came to the school and offered help to grief-stricken students and teachers trying to cope with this shocking and horrendous incident. Deanna did her best to handle the grief she was dealing with.

She located Josh's father and spoke with him on several occasions. She slept with Josh's picture for a long time. No reasons, no explanations provided an answer to the question *why*. Josh was a good student, did well on the track team, and was a kind, compassionate boy with many friends.

A life and a love lost.

Kitties

One day after school, Deanna came home with a darling, long-haired orange-and-cream-colored mostly striped kitten, which she named Butterscotch. I vaguely recall her saying something to the effect that the kitten had been abandoned by a mean old lady who hated cats, so we just had to adopt him. Deanna cried for two days, so I finally relented. We had recently moved to Newport Beach, and I was a bit hesitant about taking on any more responsibilities since we already had a sweet little silky terrier called Torie, a playful, lovable, and extremely loyal small dog. As it turned out, Torie and Butterscotch became devoted playmates. But despite her unremitting denials, it soon became evident that Deanna was allergic to cats.

Butterscotch was a wonderful cat, adoring and very handsome. He even adopted a stray feral cat our neighbor Mimi named Moochie. Mimi assumed responsibility for Moochie, seeing to it that he was neutered, had his vaccinations, and was fed. Moochie never tried to venture inside, never wanted to. It's possible he was afraid of our dog, Torie. Moochie and Butterscotch would play outside all day every day. When it started to get dark, Butterscotch came inside. Moochie always waited outside the door for him. They were inseparable. Butterscotch was Moochie's protector and sole companion.

Meanwhile, Mimi had her own indoor cat, a blue-gray Persian named Figaro. Butterscotch and Moochie used to go to Mimi's sliding glass door and taunt Figaro. This went on for a long time until one day, Mimi accidentally left her door open and Figaro escaped. Mimi was very upset and ran over to tell us. We quickly started searching for Figaro, but it proved unnecessary. We spotted the three cats walking down the street, Butterscotch in the lead, followed by Moochie and

Figaro. Butterscotch and Moochie were faithfully guiding Figaro home. It was a wonderful sight to behold, the love, respect, and trust that the three kitties had for each other—so touching to witness.

Since Butterscotch was the protector, it meant that he occasionally and unfortunately got into fights with other cats. One night, he wanted to go outside, and against my better judgment, I let him go. He was not feeling well. We had been to the veterinarian that day to take care of a wound he sustained in a fight, which had become infected. He was vulnerable, and regrettably, a coyote captured him. Moochie hung around the house for a few days, anticipating Butterscotch's return. Then he too disappeared. All of us, especially Deanna, were miserably heartbroken.

A year or two later, while vacationing in Arrowhead, we were on a hike. At one point, Deanna discovered a little kitten following us, meowing and meowing. He was a multicolored tabby that appeared to have been abandoned. We looked all over for his possible home, but our efforts were unsuccessful—and we eventually brought him back to Aunt Julie and Uncle Don's house. Laine and Deanna's cousins Jordon and Cambria were highly allergic to cats, so the little kitten had to stay outside. That night, we all stayed up and smuggled food to the kitten to entice him to stay, and sure enough, there he was right at the door early the next morning.

At the time, Deanna was raising Sabra, her puppy guide dog. Uncle Don spoke up, saying, "If Deanna has a guide dog, then Laine can have a guide cat." Laine named the cat Spencer, and he went home with us that very day.

Spencer was a very special, intelligent cat. He liked to explore the neighborhood, sometimes roaming too far from home. One day, while still relatively young, he wandered off, and we couldn't find him anywhere. Deanna made signs and posted them on trees and streetlamps in the neighborhood. Within a day or two, while searching, she heard him crying. He had climbed a tree and couldn't get down. No problem for Deanna. She immediately climbed the tree and saved Laine's rambunctious and beloved cat.

Over the years, we had more cherished cats. Smudge would sit on the fence and watch the crows taunt him. Spike looked just like Butterscotch. Willy, Fernando, and Huey were also special treasures. Allergic as Deanna was, she found it just too difficult to live without a cat. As an adult, she still was in denial about the consequences of her cat allergy, and many years later, when she was in Florida, she wanted Elle to have the experience of loving a cat as she had. And so Butterscotch II, a long-haired mostly white cat, was adopted. Sadly, it turned out that Deanna was not the only one allergic to cats; Elle was too. But there's a happy ending to this story. Butterscotch II found a new home across the country in California with me, his grandmother.

Dating

Deanna was very anxious to introduce her prized tortoise, Clyde, to Bob, a friend of mine who was visiting. She carefully handed Clyde to Bob, and he held him above his lap while admiring and complimenting him. However, Clyde apparently was not happy and unexpectedly decided to relieve himself. By the look of things, it appeared Clyde may have had a case of tortoise diarrhea. Instead of rushing to Bob's aid, we all started laughing. Poor Bob. Deanna was laughing so hard she could barely contain herself and was no help in getting Clyde back to his tortoise sanctuary. Bob quickly ran up the stairs and put Clyde in his tortoise home. Then he turned his attention to trying to clean his soiled pants. He most certainly was a good sport about the whole incident and, despite what happened, came away thinking that Deanna was a very sweet girl.

One night, my friend Ernie and I were sitting at the kitchen table, playing Scrabble. Laine and Deanna were upstairs in bed, sleeping, or so I thought. Apparently, Laine had awakened and talked Deanna into a devious plan. As Ernie and I contemplated our next Scrabble moves, there was a scream, followed immediately by a loud crash. We jumped up only to discover that the girls had tied their bedsheets together to allow Deanna to shrewdly creep over the railing from the second-story hallway so she could peek into the kitchen and see what was going on. The sheets hadn't held together. Poor Deanna took a long drop to the tile floor. And there she was, tangled up in the sheets, sitting on the floor and attempting to look totally innocent and quite surprised! Her response to the obvious question "What are you doing?" was "Nothing."

Apparently, Deanna's spying continued when Laine started dating. She was very curious, so she sometimes perched on the roof of our house with her flashlight, waiting. As soon as Laine and her date walked up to the front door, Deanna used that flashlight to put them in the spotlight for everyone in the entire neighborhood to see. No matter how frustrated and annoyed Laine was with that light dancing all around the front yard, Deanna continued spotlighting them until Laine gave up and came inside.

Eventually, Deanna started dating. That provided material for all kinds of interesting stories. Perhaps the most unusual one involved the evening Deanna met Joe, the evening she accidentally set him on fire. Joe had come to California to be an usher in Laine and Brett's wedding, and Deanna was the maid of honor. The wedding had been a beautiful affair with family and friends. Afterward, as Joe and Deanna were driving from the reception to another party, she decided to smoke a cigarette and accidentally flicked an ash onto Joe's rented tuxedo, burning a hole in it. But the hot ash didn't throw cold water on their budding relationship. Their courtship continued with hours of endless phone conversations and Joe making a trip back to California for the Christmas holidays, and then a few weeks later, Deanna moved to Florida.

CEDU

Deanna as a teenager was having problems that became cause for concern. Included were substance abuse, slipping grades, misbehavior, and dishonesty. After a two-week hospital stay to deal with some of the issues, it was recommended she attend a boarding school for the remainder of her high school years. I was forced to deal with one of the most difficult decisions I had ever faced.

I located CEDU, a beautiful school in the mountains close to our cabin in Lake Arrowhead. One story goes that the school was originally a mansion built for *Gone with the Wind* producer David O. Selznick. Another version claims it was built in the early 1930s for the Oscar-winning actor-director Walter Huston. The mountain views were spectacular, and the school had a swimming pool, a tennis court, basketball courts, and stables. It was close to ski resorts and offered mountain climbing. I thought it would be the perfect place for Deanna. To this day, I'm not sure and still have misgivings.

Deanna enrolled in CEDU toward the end of her tenth-grade year, just before her sixteenth birthday. The school's intrinsic and distinctive program was focused on the students' emotional growth. The acronym CEDU (See-Do) means "see yourself for who you are and do something with it." This was the core around which the remaining facets of the school were built, including academics, a practical work ethic, wilderness experiences, leadership, and community service training. The school was divided into five families: discovery, quest, challenge, new horizons, and source. Students advanced through each level by working on their personal issues and completing the curriculum of each individual family. CEDU was fully accredited by the Western Association of Schools and Colleges, and therefore, credits were transferable everywhere.

With the exception of higher-level math, Deanna excelled academically. She made the honor roll several times. She was picked to be a participant in the Presidential Classroom Senior High School Program. Participants enjoyed a week in Washington, DC, where they visited all the sights and took part in various activities.

CEDU had very strict rules and high expectations for all their students. Before any one of them was allowed a visit home, they were presented an outline of what they were expected to accomplish and what they were not to do. That included where the student was permitted to go, who they were allowed to see, even the music they could listen to. On one visit home, Deanna's Uncle Denny was recovering from cancer surgery. Happily, the outcome had been excellent. While we went to the hospital to visit him, Deanna said the hospital was not included in her plan. She insisted she couldn't go. I was so proud that she wanted to follow the mandated plan and rules. She was sad, however, that she couldn't go see her uncle. She stayed in the car and created a beautiful card, which remains a treasured memory for her uncle.

At CEDU, Deanna excelled in several aspects of leadership duties, attended four leadership conferences, served two terms on the House Committee, was a member of the Sports and Arts Committee, and received the Presidential Academic Fitness award. She also participated in a play, was a member of the CEDU Dance Company, and volunteered as a student tutor at a local elementary school.

At the same time, however, the emotional growth aspect of the program proved extremely difficult and demanding for Deanna. She rebelled on several occasions, even ran away twice. Occasionally, she was assigned to Full Time, which meant she would wake up, eat, write, do work assignments, and finally sleep. That encompassed her entire day. Then she'd start the whole thing all over the next day. Full Time gave the students the opportunity and space to work through negative behavior patterns. Once, she had to do it for seven days because she tried to harm herself. And because she expressed unhappiness with her appearance, Deanna was required to plant and tend to a rose garden, in addition to her other chores, all the while missing out on some of her classmates' "fun" activities.

Discovery Family Group members were charged with keeping the roads clear of snow and ice as well as chopping wood for the fireplaces. Deanna felt "they were the backbone of the school." The snow could be as deep as four and a half to six feet. Shoveling was not easy. One day, after a snowfall, she described the area, "We shoveled snow. It was really fun! It was also hard work! It's so beautiful. Everything is a vibrant white. There is also a crisp mist in the air. I love it! It's just like the song 'Winter Wonderland.' I wish you could be here with me to enjoy the beauty."

In some ways, Deanna felt she'd made progress. She wrote, "I think that in the last couple of months, I have changed a lot. I can carry on conversations and not be so sarcastic or negative. I am also having an easier time being honest. And I also think that I am more enjoyable to be around." But in the following letter, she penned, "I feel like I haven't changed one bit! I am sorry for letting you down. Yes, I know I also let others and myself down. However, I am going to do something about it."

All students at CEDU participated in wilderness training. As graduation approached, they spent five days alone in the desert. While difficult, it was designed to provide a maturing experience. It was referred to as the Solo. The students were taken to an isolated location in Joshua Tree National Park in Southern California. They had no idea the counselors and teachers were carefully supervising them from a place nearby. They were given several introspective writing assignments. A few follow:

The word *you* refers to Deanna in the following song:

> *Why are you playing such a game? Why can't you be you?*
> *Why are you trying so hard to hide the real you?*
> *Don't you see you are okay? Don't you want to be you?*
> *Now it's time to give it up. Perfection just isn't you.*
> *The desert doesn't hide its faults.*
> *It knows what it is. It's got a will to survive—just like you.*
> *Look all around, look on the ground.*
> *Everything you see is alive.*
> *Nothing is trying to hide its face. Nothing is ashamed.*
> *It accepts what it is, and it will remain.*
> *Stop playing all these stupid acceptance games.*
> *Just be you and see that you are okay.*
> *It's time for you to be who you really are,*
> *And you will be a star.*

Third Day of Solo
Solo-Third Day

Often I have sat and thought about all the ways and reasons why I should die. However, there has always been a part of me that has wanted to live. Out here, I am using that part. I don't think that I would have made it through the storm last night had I not wanted to live. I have now definitely made the choice that I want to live. I have rediscovered many marvelous values about me. Now I need to access the task of how to use them so that I have love and life.

For the desert flower, there is no question. It receives its nourishment from what I'd thought was to be my death. If such courage can grow within the fibers of such a fragile thing, then I must possess courage even stronger.

Solo
Solo-Near the End

I am having a hard time right now. I am very scared, and I miss people—most of all, I miss my mommy. I am so afraid. I hate being alone. People say that they loved Solo. Sure, I feel proud and all because I am still alive and I am courageous, but I don't like to be alone. I really don't know why. All I know is I am scared. I need someone to hold me. I feel foolish because I am seventeen years old but I am scared.

Solo—Last Day
Solo-Last Day

There is such serenity to silence. It's very comforting. It's so relaxing. I like to hear the bird chirping every so often and then hear the twang of the rabbit. Nature is a marvel, just as I am. Two separate entities yet so alike. We share the common bonds of beauty and life.

Planning Another Trip

I want the trip to go with love. I want people, including myself, to be kind to one another.

Graduation

I want people to see me as though I made a difference. I want people to know my past and accept it because I have changed. I also want people to see me as a creative individual who has struggles but is so strong; she can do anything. I want to be seen as beautifully unique, a free thinker, and someone who voices her opinions. I want to be seen as I am, living life to its fullest. I want people to see me as a friend by being a friend.

Thoughts

I am learning to be happy where I am,
I am learning that locked with the moments
of each day are all the joys,
The peace, the fibers of the cloth we call life . . .
The meaning is in the moment—
There is no other way to find it.
You feel what you allow yourself to feel,
Each and every moment of the day!

The Ocean

Sand and sun are so wonderful. I love snuggling up with the sand. Plus, I love exploring. The water is forgiving. You can put anything in it, and it still forgives you and tries to cleanse itself. It lets people play in it, and it lets people travel in it. In some ways, I am like the ocean. People have done wrong to me and I have hurt people, but I accept it and do my best to move on. Maybe that's why I'm here, to be like the tide and cleanse myself and get rid of the false impurities. Be me—free, innocent, pure, and alive. When I graduate, I definitely have to live at the beach. Sand and sun are so wonderful.

Deanna worked exceptionally hard at CEDU, graduated, and prepared to attend Northern Arizona University in the fall.

Deanna: Almost Lost in Australia

Deanna and her then-boyfriend Simon, an Olympic pole-vaulter, loved sports of all kinds and welcomed most athletic challenges. But no challenge, none, compared to their treacherous experience while white-water rafting near the Great Barrier Reef in Australia.

It was an extremely cold, rainy, and windy day—not the best time to go rafting. Nonetheless, they decided to go because they had a reservation and might not get another chance. Both of them were excellent swimmers, so they weren't worried. Rafting was just too exciting to let the weather stop them. Once in the raft, however, they weren't so sure. Deanna and Simon were in front, and three people were seated behind them. They were paddling as hard as they could in the wild white water, when suddenly they lost control and the raft completely overturned. Everyone was tossed into the water. Soon, four of the rafters surfaced, but where was Deanna? Simon thought the worst. Several scary minutes went by before someone finally spotted her clinging to a boulder. By this time, Deanna was far from their raft and had to be rescued by another rafter. She was pretty banged up but thankful—and lucky—to be alive.

Australia is a beautiful big country consisting of one huge island and over eight thousand small ones. One day, we took a ferry over to Kangaroo Island. We were accompanied by dolphins swimming and playing alongside the boat, showing off how cute and friendly they can be. Kangaroo Island is known for its beautiful beaches and interesting rock formations, many of which are covered with brilliant-orange lichen, offering magnificent contrasts to the bright blue sky. Of course, the island has an abundant population of kangaroos, wallabies, and koalas. The latter were usually seen munching away on the leaves of eucalyptus trees. Simon was full of stories about the Tasmanian devil. He really wanted Deanna to see one. The devils are about the size of a large dog, with mostly black fur, a pungent odor, and an ear-splitting, horrible-sounding screech. They love carrion and will eat anything, no matter how rotten it is. They're the largest carnivorous marsupials in the world. Not pretty, they're scary looking, especially when their mouths are open and they're eating. Luckily, we didn't see any in the wild but did see them in a fenced enclosure. Tasmanian devils are found only in Australia.

Australia is home to twenty-one of the twenty-five deadliest snakes in the world. The fierce snake, also known as the inland taipan, is said to be the deadliest snake in the world. A few others of Australia's most venomous are the brown tree snake, the tiger, the Eastern tiger, and the death adder. Although none of us ever came across any of these in the wild, Simon constantly entertained us with horror stories and tales about how dangerous and scary they were. We were especially cautious and never ventured into tall grassy areas.

Thankfully, there were the sweet little koalas and the kangaroos, some of which were so tame that they could be petted.

Australia. It was an outstanding trip!

Kayaking at the Great Barrier Reef

The Fashionista

Whatever the circumstances, some people just have the ability to always look perfect. They seem to know how to dress for any occasion. Deanna was one of those people. Not only did she know what looked good on her but she also had the ability to assess the appearance of others and assist them in finding the right item of clothing or the perfect accessory to accentuate their attributes while minimizing any flaws. Her skills were instinctive.

Deanna worked hard to keep up with the latest designers and the current trends. She devoured every fashion magazine she could get her hands on, was fascinated with the history of style, and studied fashion in college.

Our friend and neighbor Bobi frequented some boutiques where Deanna worked in Newport Beach. All these years later, when Bobi looks in her closet, she's reminded of a special afternoon when Deanna convinced her to buy a beautiful suit for work. The suit is still in her closet, a split-second reminder of Deanna.

One of Deanna's favorite jobs was working as a sales associate at Gucci in Bal Harbour, Florida. This boutique is a very high-end establishment. Deanna earned the confidence of many customers, who trusted her taste in selections and even made purchases sight unseen based on her recommendations. Some of her clients lived in Europe and South America and only vacationed in Florida sporadically throughout the year and in winter. They depended on her suggestions to look wealthy and prestigious, to fit in to the area's high-society scene. Deanna never let them down.

Deanna was also skilled with makeup. She knew how to emphasize a person's best features while downplaying any imperfections. At Laine and Brett's wedding, being the mother of the bride, I was extremely nervous. In the chaos of the bridesmaids and the bride getting ready, Deanna calmly did my makeup. It took her a while, but to this day, I'm told that I never looked better.

The Perfect Sounding Board

Laine Kontos Oberst

My last conversation with Deanna—and one of my most memorable—happened a few days before she died. It was about contact lenses!

On Tuesday, April 5, I sent Deanna a text message, stating, "At the eye doctor's office getting an exam and being fitted for contact lenses! Yea!" Uncharacteristically, Deanna called me back immediately. Even before I could get out a hello, she was yelling, "Are you crazy? Get out of there! What are you doing? Don't you remember what happened last time? I had to put those things in for you, and you almost passed out! In fact, you practically passed out just watching me put my own contacts in." (To back up a bit, ten years earlier, I got contacts for my wedding with disastrous results. Deanna literally had to pin me down and put them in my eyes. And once in, the contacts appeared to exaggerate my crossed eyes. So I just wore them on my wedding day.)

I assured her that this time would be different. And by *assure*, I yelled, "It will be different this time! That was long ago!" The doctor then came in, and we ended our conversation.

On April 8, I went back to the doctor's office to pick up my contacts and take my "contact lens class." Two hours later, I still was unable to put in the contacts. Finally, the nurse put them in for me. I glanced in a mirror only to see that both eyes were completely crossed. The doctor popped in and said that with my eye condition, that was a very common response and the reason many people can't wear contacts. I felt that little bit of information might have been beneficial to know earlier in the process.

I left the office very upset, convinced that it was all Deanna's fault, that Deanna had somehow jinxed me. I called and yelled into her voicemail for about five minutes. Later, I found out that when Deanna listened to the message, she smiled, laughed, then laughed some more. She told her boyfriend, "I'm keeping this one." And she did. She listened to my message a few more times that day, each time laughing and laughing.

This was just one of many instances illustrating Deanna's ability to be an amazing sounding board. She was the only person I wanted, and still want, to call when I am just so upset that I need to yell or rant a bit. She always calmed me down somehow. I would be hysterical, and she would say something like "I hear you are upset." That phrase would usually make me laugh or at least make me feel calmer. I miss this so much. I never had this relationship with anyone else, and its complete loss and absence is so, so painful.

Loving and Giving

Deanna took great pleasure in helping others. As a child and as an adult, she had an innate ability to understand people and react in a caring and compassionate way.

We had a grandmotherly neighbor nicknamed Mimi. She was slowly going blind due to macular degeneration. Deanna was of elementary school age at the time and would visit Mimi to help her with meals, on occasion feed her cat and clean his litter box, and sometimes ask her to play her organ. Mimi, in her eighties, was one of the first people we knew who had purchased a personal home computer. It was an IBM model, larger than most television sets of the time. Deanna became Mimi's eyes to a degree, assisting her in creating cards and letters, word puzzles, and short rhymes. She described Mimi once as "having that lap I could curl up on . . . a shoulder to cry on, and was always there to comfort me whenever I felt down. She was a very important person in my life." When Deanna was about ten years old, she planned a surprise birthday party for Mimi at our house. Mimi was astounded and exceedingly happy.

Luckily, we had a large backyard, because Deanna was continually bringing home lost dogs. Some had collars with identifying information, some didn't. It was easy to track down the owners whose dogs had current addresses and phone numbers on their tags, but not so for others. For those dogs, Deanna would go knocking on all the doors near where the dog had been found, put up Dog Found signs, and ask everyone she saw if they had any information regarding the dog. Needless to say, we had lots of dog guests at our house. In every case, Deanna's tenacity led to the dog's owner.

Both girls were in elementary school when we visited New York. What a fabulous and fun experience! One day, while walking in front of Rockefeller Plaza and passing a hot dog stand, I tripped, landing *splat* on the sidewalk. There were lots of people around, most of them just staring. Laine looked at me, made sure I was alive, and then ran way ahead of us to avoid embarrassment. I made the most of the situation, pretending I couldn't get up without my glasses or maybe my "broken foot." Deanna stayed with me and tried to help. She said I was acting "wacko," but she wouldn't leave my side no matter how absurd I acted. I was just fine, thoroughly savoring the very different responses of my daughters.

As a seventh-grade teacher, I was aware that some of my students had eating disorders. Deanna volunteered to speak to all 160 boys and girls in a special assembly. Her ability to hold the attention of junior high school children was phenomenal. She spoke honestly about her own eating disorder and offered possible methods of coping should they or any of their friends encounter such a problem. Many students stayed after the assembly and spoke with her at length.

Deanna liked to give presents, and she gave lots of them. It almost hurt thinking about how giving she was, especially when there were many times she couldn't afford to be so generous. One memorable gift was a portrait of both her and Laine she commissioned to have painted. I had always yearned for one to put in the living room. Another special gift was a book she bought and filled in mostly with her personal thoughts. The book was titled *Mother, Thank You For . . .*

Bobi finds herself giggling when remembering the winter day the tall, graceful old pepper tree in front of their house, with an abundant mass of dark-green foliage, fell after a heavy rainfall, blocking the street. The city had come and had started sawing the trunk into logs about the size of firewood, cleaning up leaves and branches, when Deanna showed up. She was carrying a little ficus tree in a one-gallon container. She announced, bursting with laughter, "Here is your new tree!" Well, that tree remains planted in the side yard, and every time Deanna visited it, she always laughed. Bobi and her husband, Jock, always thought it was so special that Deanna actually stopped at a nursery and bought them a tree in the hope that they would recover from their loss. The Deanna tree thrives to this day and now serves as a remembrance of her.

After her freshman year at Northern Arizona University, Deanna was offered a job by two of her previous high school teachers. They were starting a new school for troubled children in Georgia and wanted Deanna to live in a dorm with about seven girls as a "counselor, friend, and mentor." She'd be able to attend North Georgia College, which was fairly close to the school, allowing her to continue her education. However, the job ended up being extremely detrimental both emotionally and physically for Deanna. She simply was not trained or prepared for the complexities involving teenagers with serious psychological disorders, most of them being on medication. She stayed not quite a year. Although there rather briefly, her dorm girls and boys wrote her many letters after she left. Among them are as follows:

I'm going to miss you. You were a big part of my work and progress here. There were times when I was ready to just quit, but you were the reason why I didn't. You took a dorm with a bunch of rooms and turned it into one of the safest and most comfortable homes that I have ever lived in. You brought a strong sense of safety to my life here at HLA. Even on the worst days, I could always count on you to cure my sadness. You gave me some harsh feedback, and I always made sure to listen because I truly believed it was coming from your heart or personal experience. I am so sorry for the times I was mean to you or threw shoes at you or even slammed doors in your face. I never meant to hurt you. You have always been special to me. It finally came to the point where I had to be protective of you and not share you with everyone else. . . . You will always be in my heart. I will think of you every day. I learned more from our one-on-one conversations than anything else this school has taught me.

I am thankful for the time we had. It seems as soon as people walked into my life, they were walking out. I am scared to get close to anyone . . . my parents were too wrapped up in their own lives to care about me.

I see you through my window of despair. I see your sunshine. You shine on everyone, pretty much everywhere . . . although we are going to be out of reaching distance, when I bring myself back from my darkness, I shall think of your face and hopefully I can climb over your rainbow, and maybe I will be happy again. Because you, you are a friend.

I love you and I don't want you to leave this school.

There is one present that I don't give very often, and I only give it to people who are special to me. It is the gift of honesty, friendship, and faith. I want to give this to you because you mean so much to me.

It is so hard to see you leave. I could write a novel on how hard it is as you mean so much to me.

And one very troubled student wrote the following:

I am feeling really sad, and I am having dreams about when my friend got shot and how I shot that kid, and it scares me . . . I'm scared I won't see you again and that you'll forget about me . . . Thank you for being my friend, Deanna.

Deanna received many loving testimonials not just from her mentees but from friends and family as well.

Deanna's stepmother, Connie, was having problems with Deanna's dad. One day, Connie was sitting outside their home in her old Peugeot (that's a car!), and Deanna came and sat with her, offering support and wisdom. Connie felt Deanna wanted her to know that she was complete with or without a man in her life. "Deanna had a spirit of encouragement and recognized the wounded when she saw them. She had a strong core, and when she was encouraging someone, she was at her very best. All the rebellion and anger was put aside, and she was pure love."

Her cousin Denise described Deanna's gift simply: "She took care of people, but when it came to taking care of herself, it was harder. . . . She had an impact on each and every one of us."

A woman who lost her twenty-one-year-old son suddenly and tragically was inspired by Deanna's caring heart. She told Denise that Deanna called her every day to remind her that someone loved her.

Kristin wrote of Deanna:

> I can always remember looking up to Deanna as a young girl would look up to her bigger sister. I saw her as a free-spirited, fun, and beautiful person, and those were the qualities I admired about Deanna throughout her life. She had a way with people . . . I can remember being a freshman in high school, a young, awkward adolescent. I was so excited for Deanna to teach me a dance that I could use during tryouts for the school's dance team. Although I completely blanked out at the tryouts due to nerves and didn't end up making the team, I had no regrets about going through the process. I had so much fun dancing around the house with Deanna, laughing together and feeling like I could just be myself during a very difficult and unsure phase of my life. I never felt judged, and Deanna was so proud of me even though I didn't make the team. She was the type of person that glowed in social settings and brought a smile to everyone's face with her contagious laugh. I will never forget her positive outlook on life and how she made me feel about myself.

A New Baby Coming

Dear Grandma,

I am so excited to share my great news with you. Joe and I are pregnant! My emotions are running wild. Mostly, I am grateful to be blessed with this joyful gift. Also, I am so proud that you will know and love your new great-grandbaby. If you have any guidance you would like to enlighten me with, I'd truly appreciate it. I believe I am about eight weeks along. My doctor's appointment is December 18. I will give you more details then.

I love you.

Love,
Deanna

Dear Deanna,

What exciting news! I'm overwhelmed. Just think—first, Cindy and now, you—a double dose of great-grandmotherhood in one year, 2003. I am so lucky. I know you are very happy, and I am very, very happy for you!

As far as any guidance to give, you are already very capable and knowledgeable. I am certain you already know all the right rules to follow in order to handle this new life and great responsibility and will have a happy and healthy baby.

Everything will be fine! You will do a great job and handle this superbly.

Congratulations and love,
Grandma and Great-Grandma to be!

Cynthia and Deanna were pregnant at about the same time. They spoke about how exciting it was to be pregnant and be the first out of all their generation to have babies and make their grandma a great-grandma. As it turned out, Elle and Dylan were born just a few months apart, both on the twenty-third of the month—Dylan in January and Elle in July.

Deanna's grandmother, whom everyone loved and adored, is the mother of four children, the grandmother of fifteen grandchildren, and in 2003, her first great-grandchildren were born. And as of 2013, twelve more have followed.

Life Change

Pregnancy changed everything. Eating properly and not drinking or smoking are things most women will accomplish without major effort in pursuit of a healthy pregnancy. That would not be easy for Deanna, battling several addictions, but she did it! She transformed completely, devoting herself to doing everything possible to ensure a pregnancy without complications that would result in the birth of a healthy baby. Cancel the very slim figure Deanna maintained throughout her life. Her anorexic and bulimic behaviors practically disappeared as she happily gained quite a bit of weight. Deanna's focus was solely on her baby. As it turned out, her pregnancy proved to be about the healthiest time of her life, at least since age thirteen or fourteen.

Never having been an enthusiastic reader, Deanna nonetheless devoured every book she could find about pregnancy and child care. She took infant first-aid classes all in preparation to be the best possible mother. She and Joey went to every doctor's appointment together and followed all medical advice. Deanna wanted Joey's mother and his sister, Jody, take an infant CPR course. Both of them had raised three children, and Jody was a registered nurse—yet they happily completed the course.

As Deanna's due date approached, it appeared that her baby girl was not ready to make an appearance. Hoping to encourage the birth, Deanna and I walked and walked up and down the shoreline at the Marriott Resort and Spa in Florida. Nothing happened. We tried swimming; still, nothing happened. The doctor finally decided to induce labor, so off we went to the hospital. Joe was carrying pillows in preparation for labor, a how-to book, and other necessary supplies. Deanna carried a huge smile on her face. She and Joey had taken the hospital predelivery course and were well prepared. Nevertheless, after many, many hours of difficult labor, Deanna and her doctor became impatient. Deanna was upset with her dad for bringing lox and bagels of every flavor, including onion and cheese, into the labor room. The smell made her nauseous. In an effort to alleviate a tense situation, he hid all the food in the bathroom. Laine and Brett took off, spending the day floating on rafts in the pool, but they were back in time for the birth after a few pleasant hours of relaxation. Brett also managed to put together a portable crib for his soon-to-be little niece.

Finally, Elle Marie Paglino was born by Cesarean section at 7:06 p.m.—a healthy, happy, beautiful baby girl with big blue eyes. We were all overjoyed. Elle weighed seven pounds two ounces and was nineteen inches tall. And she scored 9 on the Apgar scale, which assesses the health of the baby immediately after birth. Elle, just like her mommy, was uncommonly alert for a newborn and had lots of straight brown hair. Deanna and Joe were filled with pride and were absolutely elated. We grandparents were beyond thrilled and kept congratulating each other and the parents while admiring the cutest baby girl ever!

Visiting Elle in the hospital was not easy. There were guards at the door, and each visitor had to have identification. Then you were given a badge and a wristband with your name on it, and you had to have it with you at all times. They were determined that no one would swipe little Elle. Aunt Laine and Uncle Brett's identification badges are presently hanging on the water heater at Elle's home.

Losing her pregnancy weight took Deanna about a year, but she did it in a healthy way, primarily because she was determined to nurse her baby for at least nine months, which she accomplished. To Deanna, the birth of her daughter was, without a doubt, the highlight of her life.

The big day has arrived!

Deanna's Advice

When Laine became pregnant with her first child, it was Deanna's advice and experience that proved to be more helpful than anyone else's. Deanna seemed to know everything about pregnancy, from what one should eat in the various trimesters to the level and type of fitness that was ideal for a mom-to-be. This was not a surprise, considering the amount of research she had done throughout her pregnancy with Elle. As a parent, Deanna also developed very unusual yet extremely effective methods of handling difficult situations when it came to caring for a newborn and toddler.

One unconventional yet very effective piece of advice she shared with Laine was her use of various creative gimmicks or tricks as a way of diffusing temper tantrums. As Elle would cry and scream, Deanna would distract her with all kinds of questions or imitate her behavior in that moment. Each time, they would both end up laughing, with the tantrum immediately forgotten. Deanna might ask, "Elle, which room would you be more comfortable crying in? Or how much longer do you think you are going to cry? Can you cry a little louder? Would some water help?" Other times, she imitated Elle, saying and then demonstrating, "This is how you look when you are crying," and would follow by making the funniest faces, sometimes adding a nearby prop to further dramatize the situation. Deanna was naturally an animated person, so this was priceless—and they would both end up laughing hysterically. These little tips were probably the best bit of parenting wisdom that Deanna passed on to Laine, who is now a mother of two little girls, three and five, and uses these techniques regularly.

Deanna made being a mom look fun and easy mostly because she was truly having fun and was experiencing the best years of her life being Elle's mom.

The Key Chain

Joe Paglino

Mommy never let you wear a bathing suit or diaper at the beach when you were a baby. She was worried your chubby legs would get a rash from the sand getting stuck in your suit. Plus, it made going to the bathroom a lot easier. One October weekend, we were vacationing in Bonita Springs. It was your fist trip to the Coconut Plantation Resort. We took a boat across the bay to a private beach. Mommy was not about to show off what she considered her postpregnancy floppy tushy; hence, she wore sweatpants. Both of you giggled as you played in the surf. As much as Mommy loved to watch you play, she loved holding you even more.

Not long after the trip, Mommy bought a key chain with an attachment for holding pictures. She thought this was the perfect way to quell her insatiable desire to always have you with her. As soon as she got home with her new gift, she began searching through our voluminous pictures of you to find the perfect ones to fill the insets. She picked her favorite ten and trimmed them to fit.

The key chain looked ridiculous. It was bulky and flopped around whenever she held her keys, but she never took the pictures off the key chain—ever. This became a point of contention, because when I would drive us somewhere in Mommy's car, I had to fit this portable album in my pocket. I tried convincing Mommy to disconnect the pictures, but she refused. Having you close to her was more important.

After a few years, people who saw the key chain would ask Mommy why she didn't update the pictures. To strangers, it seemed like she had a year-old baby because none of the pictures showed you growing up.

Of all her accomplishments, Mommy was most proud of being your mother. The pictures were a daily reminder of the greatest day of her life—the day you were born. While the edges of the pictures wore down from constant jostling as she fumbled with her keys over the next six years, the memory of her love for you was as sharp and clear as the day she first played with you in the surf.

Elle's First Trip to Disney World

Joe Paglino

Since the moment you were born, I counted the days until you were old enough to visit Disney World. Simultaneously, Mommy had been dreading that day. She and Aunt Laine shared a distaste for Disney, one they were all too willing to share with others. You have to understand. They grew up by Disneyland—the older, smaller, tackier version of Disney World. She just didn't understand how awesome Disney could be. Finally, after two and one-half years of waiting, I guilt-tripped your mommy into going. With the new camera we gave her for Mother's Day a week earlier, we were off for some Disney magic. This being your first visit, we took more pictures than all our later trips put together.

To convince Mommy Disney had a sophisticated side, we stopped at the Grand Floridian Resort on the way to the Magic Kingdom. This was the fanciest hotel in Disney World. If anything could persuade Mommy that Disney wasn't a dilapidated day care for screaming kids, it was this hotel. The viability of future visits hung in the balance. As we approached the entrance, we saw a beautiful white car from the 1930s displayed outside, exuding the opulence that waited inside. She loved the car and the resort. Most of all, she loved making you happy.

Mommy endured a weekend of crowds, lines, and Florida heat. It was torture for her, but through it all, she kept smiling because she knew you were enjoying yourself. It's a Small World was your favorite ride. You would jump up and down in your seat and gaze—with mouth agape—at the singing characters. We went on it so many times we all memorized the song.

Mommy was convinced you would get lost or kidnapped as we walked through the parks, so she carried you nearly the entire weekend. If not hanging like a monkey on her back, you were in her arms.

Although we've been to Disney dozens of times since then, none of our subsequent trips could match the excitement and joy you had discovering Disney for the first time with your mommy.

Flower Girls

Deanna was seven when her Aunt Chrissy and Uncle Steve married in 1982. She was their flower girl, sprinkling flower petals down the aisle with pride and personality. She was missing her two front teeth, but her smile was endearing.

Many years later, Elle followed in her mother's footsteps, being the perfect flower girl twice. Michele and Cambria, both cousins of Deanna, were married when Elle was the perfect flower girl age.

Michele and Andreas were married in Lake Arrowhead, California. Michele's sister, Cynthia, remembers how Deanna repeatedly encouraged Elle not to be nervous about walking down the aisle. Deanna kept telling Elle how pretty she looked, saying over and over how much she loved her. Cynthia recalled, "It was so sweet to see her dedication to her daughter and how Elle looked to her mother for encouragement before taking that walk."

Michele's mother wrote Elle the following letter:

Dear Elle,

Do you remember when you were the flower girl in cousin Michele and Andreas's wedding? I do. I will never forget the love that flowed between you and your mom on that day. Before the ceremony, she came upstairs where the wedding party was, scooped you up into her arms, and hugged and kissed you. She told you how beautiful you looked and how much she loved you. This same scene was repeated immediately after the wedding, where you dutifully scattered rose petals in the path of the bride. No one could have done it better, and your mom was there to let you know that. Once again, she "loved you up." You were definitely the love of her life. It was a beautiful bond that I witnessed that day.

With love,
Aunt Gaby

Cambria and Logan's wedding followed soon after in Malibu, California. Cambria, Deanna, and Elle had gone shopping in Florida to look at both bridal and flower girl dresses. Cambria recalled going to a boutique where there were many, many dresses hanging, and smashed in the middle was a hot-pink wedding dress. Elle spotted it and gasped, "Wow! Cam! It's . . . *beautiful*! You should get this one!"

Cambria thought Elle was a little disappointed when they left empty-handed. Several bridal shops later, Elle was especially excited to try on one particular dress. She was so cute! She practiced a bunch of twirls in front of all the mirrors and tried on flower veils too. She was extremely excited. Her face was glowing, and by default, so was Deanna's. The remembrance of Deanna beaming at Elle and her twirling remain impressed in Cambria's mind.

At the wedding rehearsal, Elle, only five at the time, was taking her job very seriously. She was concerned that Cambria wasn't standing in the exact right spot in the midst of the wedding party. Cambria assured her that it would be okay if she wasn't directly behind the person in front of her. Elle's response was, 'Cam, you're not taking this wedding seriously enough!" Cambria and all her bridesmaids thought Elle's comment especially hilarious, which it was!

On the day of the wedding, Elle sat perfectly still while the hairdresser curled and pinned up her hair. She followed directions and was the most beautiful flower girl ever!

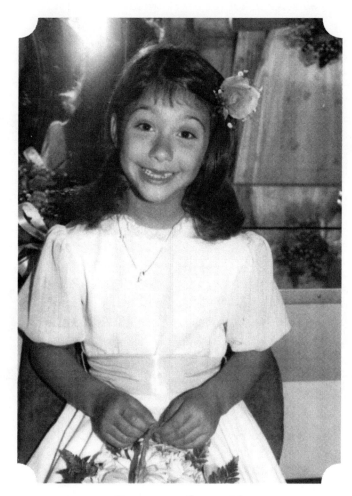

Deanna as a flower girl

Joe and Deanna
Proud Parents

An Exercise Instructor

Climbing out of her crib at barely nine months of age, falling on her head, and then doing it again two minutes later was my first clue that Deanna was extremely well coordinated, athletic, strong, and daring. And she was! Throughout her life, she was passionate about sports and fitness and was always willing to try almost any new athletic endeavor.

In elementary school, soccer became Deanna's passion. Usually, she played goalie, and very few players could score on her. She was kicked about the face and head many times. It got to the point where I could barely watch when the ball was headed toward the goal. As it turned out, Deanna suffered an ankle injury in her first semester at college, which ended her soccer career.

She then pursued running, swimming, and cycling. Her love of sports led her to the exercise field. She became a personal trainer and taught body toning and cycling classes mostly at the YMCA and at various gyms in the area. At one point, she even started her own exercise business. Her classes were always full. She would give her students small motivational gifts for the holidays, call those who missed class, and did many extra things that made her students feel valued.

The following was written by Maria Hagg, one of Deanna's students:

> I only knew Deanna for a short time, maybe five years or so, but the impact she had on my life will be forever. She was my first serious spin instructor at the YMCA in Hollywood, Florida. I landed in her class one Monday morning by sheer accident. She introduced herself to me, and everybody was laughing, telling me that I didn't know what I was getting myself into. She told everyone to "shush up" and promptly

told me she was excited to see a new face. I remember smiling (I think!) but being very nervous looking at her! I thought her body was *peeeerrrrfect*! And was I going to make it through this class? She helped me set up my bike and asked where my water was. I didn't have any but assured her I would be fine. She gave me this smile, went to her bag, got out a single dollar bill, and said to go and get one and that she would wait for me before she started the class. She didn't even *know me*! *How nice!* I thought. From then on, I was a nut to make every class. As a side note to that first encounter, the following Monday, I made sure I had a dollar to give back to her. Her response, of course, was "Keep it and give it to someone else one day who might need some water."

She brought with her this wonderful sense of well-being only to be knitted together with a fierce determination to get things done the right way or not at all. It was hard keeping up with her, and that's what I loved about her so much. She had incredible discipline when it came to all things fitness.

To this day, *nobody* comes close to how Deanna taught spin. I haven't taken a spin class yet and not thought of her. Everybody tells me I have the best form while spinning. I'm so proud to say that Deanna taught me. I so miss her.

Deanna truly enjoyed working in the exercise field but, after a few years, wanted to try other careers.

Thanksgiving Flowers

Deanna was a very spiritual person.

She treasured her family and her friends. Holidays were always very special. They were a time to enjoy and appreciate loved ones. One Thanksgiving holiday, Deanna and her boyfriend, Steve, were on their way to a friend's home in Florida for an anticipated scrumptious dinner and conversation.

But Deanna had a secret plan. She insisted on leaving early for dinner. It was unusual because she tended to run late much of the time. In South Florida, you'll frequently see vendors on street corners selling holiday gifts, particularly flowers. Riding along, Deanna suddenly got very excited and started punching Steve on the shoulder, demanding that he pull over as they drove close to a street vendor. She jumped out of the car and headed directly for the vendor. She came back carrying an armful of flowers and requested thirty dollars from Steve. He thought it was a little excessive, but well . . . okay.

"I wish I could describe how Deanna's smile, along with her enthusiasm, won the argument. It was something about the way she smiled when she wanted something. It may have been the way she slightly nodded her head or the expression in her eyes," recalled Steve. "She was not going to take no for an answer."

Steve logically assumed she wanted to bring them to Thanksgiving dinner, but why so many flowers? They had six bouquets. He kept questioning why so many flowers were necessary, but headstrong Deanna would not explain. Steve was not happy about it, but he did love and trust her. So he just drove on, all the time wondering what Deanna was up to. She directed him to a nearby cemetery. They parked and got out with five of the bouquets. "Today is about family and friends," Deanna told him.

The two of them spent the next half hour walking around the cemetery, stopping and placing a few of the flowers at the grave sites that were bare. As she placed a flower on each one, she said a little prayer.

A Company
Boating Party

Ralph Pokorny

In 2010, our company, Restorations Xperts, was on a roll. Things with the company were going well, and we decided to celebrate with a company outing aboard a seventy-foot catamaran out of Fort Lauderdale. It was in July, and the weather was hot though bearable. We invited all the staff of our company and included their family and friends. There were about sixty-five people on board, and everyone was in a good mood. We were prepared to have a great time.

The sail was to consist of a ride offshore, where we would eventually stop, dropping anchor, and then snorkel around the local reefs. We headed off but noticed there was a storm far in the distance. There was no telling exactly where it was headed; however, living in Florida, we all know that storms can come and go, and they are typically localized. This day was a bit different. The sea started to kick up, and even though the boat was quite large and stable, there were some weak stomachs in the group; and as the storm got closer, several of the passengers were getting quite green about the gills. Deanna was having a great time. She was talking with everyone on the boat; though she only had known a few, she made her usual impact. She got to meet everyone. This was good to see as being the host of the party, I was hoping that the number of green passengers would be far outweighed by the number of happy campers. The ratio was pretty good, but a few seasick passengers can dampen the mood of the party. Having experienced seasickness in the past, I had a lot of empathy for the "ill ones." It's not consoling for a seasick guest to be observing the laughing and howling of those that have the good fortune of being blessed with strong stomachs while they lie down, covering their faces and believing that this might be their last day on the planet.

The captain, in his wisdom, decided to go back to the intracoastal and implement plan B, which was a sail around New River followed by anchoring in a relatively secluded spot. The water was brackish, and the current pretty swift. After anchoring the boat, the captain inflated a large round raft and tethered it to the boat with a one-hundred-foot line. Guests could swim back and forth from the boat to the raft. Lots of fun! Everyone that had been seasick was feeling better now that the waters were still, so the mood was full of enjoyment. People began swimming and floating downstream to the raft. However, some of them had difficulty getting back to the boat as they were not strong-enough swimmers to go against the current. Now, this was not just one or two people but perhaps a dozen.

Deanna, seeing the struggling guests, dove in the water and began to shuttle the swimmers back to the boat. It was amazing. She swam effortlessly back and forth, bringing one person at a time with her, all the while with her typical grin. She swam like a fish—but not just like any fish. She swam with the grace of a sailfish. Her long, slender body just moved through the water seemingly without effort.

Back and forth she went. She was the shuttle, and she thought nothing of it. When she finally got out of the water, she just continued with her smile. I complimented her and thanked her, and she dismissed my words. She just acted like it was no big deal and that she was just happy to be of help.

Deanna always smiled. She was continually giving out compliments, and she was regularly offering her help. She had her way of dealing with people. She could make you feel special. That was who she was, and that's why she was so loved.

Insights into Empathy

When Deanna was just a toddler, my friend Wendy and I used to take our daughters with us while we'd jog at the local high school track. The three children would play in the center of the track so we could keep an eye on them. It was fun for the girls, and it gave us time to visit while we exercised. Occasionally, we became concerned when other runners allowed their dogs to run loose on the field because Deanna just could not resist running after them, wanting to play. Luckily, there was never a problem.

One hot and windy day, fires had broken out, threatening many homes in the surrounding mountains. From the track, the flames and smoke were clearly visible. After being reassured the fire was not near their homes, the two older girls continued playing, disregarding the potential danger of the situation. Deanna, however, was very distressed and worried about all the animals that might not be able to escape. We did our best to reassure her that the firefighters were there and that all the animals would be saved. Three decades later, Wendy recalled, "Deanna was worrying with tears in her eyes. When I think of her, her love and caring always comes to my mind."

Our neighbors Bobi and Jock had Goda, a beautiful Doberman pinscher. As a teenager, Deanna loved to take Goda with her on runs. Goda, eagerly anticipating a run, would, on many occasions, be found waiting in their courtyard for Deanna to come home from school or work. Deanna thought it was funny when she earned the nickname "Goda's girlfriend." Then Boris was adopted as a companion for Goda. Although Boris was aggressive, our neighbors thought he would outgrow it with love and training. Deanna would go over some evenings to pet the dogs and chat, often for hours. Her hands would get extremely dirty—almost black—from the deep massaging she gave both dogs. Unfortunately, one day, Boris bit Jock's hand, and they decided they'd have to return him to the Doberman rescue organization. The night before they took him back, Deanna spent a good two or three hours petting him, crying that Boris was being sent away. It was a very sad night for everyone.

Some years later, Deanna and her cousin Ben spent a day snowboarding in Big Bear. It was one of those perfect days. Well, almost perfect. While they were on a chairlift slowly ascending the mountain, there was a ski patrol rescuer speeding underneath them, towing an injured skier to the first-aid station. Deanna grabbed Ben's hand and screamed, "Quick, quick, close your eyes! We need to send him our positive thoughts."

Deanna's cousin Cynthia had a friend who eventually played professional soccer with the Anaheim Ducks. He had given Cynthia free tickets, and she invited Deanna to go to a game with her. Cynthia, usually quiet and reserved, was excited and clapped when her friend scored, but that was about all. Deanna turned to her and said, "Is that all you've got, Squid?" (It was Cynthia's nickname.) So Deanna took over. She got up, waving her hands and cheering loudly, "Way to go, Armando. You've got it, Armando."

Cynthia was surprised. "She didn't even know Armando. It was hilarious. I was so proud because as a result, my friend got his fan club that he so desperately needed and wanted. I just couldn't provide that for him."

After Elle was born, Joe and Deanna were very fortunate to find an exceptional nanny, so Deanna was able to go back to work. But after only a few months, their nanny, Marlene, had to return home. Deanna was quite upset and wrote to me, "Yesterday, we were both crying. Marlene is going home to Bolivia. All I know is that I am so sad. Elle and I have totally fallen in love with her. I am selfishly sad for myself as well as sad for Marlene. Her son, in Bolivia, was finally approved to come here; however, he is taking care of a family member there who is quite ill. So now Marlene must return to Bolivia to enable her son to come here. She told me that of all the jobs and homes that she has worked in, ours was her favorite. She said that I treat her as family and she loves Joe, Elle, and me. I am so grateful to know her. She is a great woman, and I will miss her so much." Deanna and Joe never did find a nanny that could even begin to replace Marlene.

A few years ago, I stopped seeing Jerry, a person I had been dating. No one but Deanna could tell that I was sad about the breakup, and Deanna lived many miles away. It was the way she said "I'm so sorry, Mom" that was so special to me. I still feel those words. She understood my sorrow more than anyone else.

About five months into her second pregnancy, Cynthia experienced some bleeding. The doctor ordered immediate bed rest. Deanna heard about it and called her. "She was so upset about the thought of something bad happening to the baby that it brought her to immediate tears," Cynthia recalled. "She kept crying, 'Squid, what happened?' Deanna knew firsthand the bond that exists between mother and child. She put herself in my shoes and could feel my fear and pain herself. That was just Deanna being Deanna."

Laine and her close friend and roommate Tim had just graduated from law school. Naturally, they were very excited, but before they could practice law in California, they first had to take and pass the state bar exam. Studying for the exam is extremely grueling. Passing it is far from easy. Approximately half the law students who take it don't pass it on their first try. Deanna was exuberant when she learned Laine had passed it. Unfortunately, Tim did not. When he came to our house to tell us the bad news, Deanna tried anything she could to ease the disappointment. She brought out drinks and appetizers and told Tim how sorry she was, offering him lots of encouragement for the next time he'd take the test. And the next time, he passed it.

Throughout her life, Deanna was affected and moved by others. She had deep, deep feelings and did her best to help everyone she could.

More than anything, though, Deanna loved being a mother. She lavished Elle with affection. I was watching one day as they went jogging. Elle, in her stroller, was having a wonderful time. When she started to scramble out, Deanna couldn't wait to hug and kiss her. They rolled on the grass, laughing and tickling each other.

Neighborhood Friends

Carrie Petrucione and Adelle,
Enoch, and Judah McGowan

My first memory of meeting Deanna was hearing her yell "Elllllllllllllllllle." She had such a distinct voice; her tone was rich, and her voice was powerful, with the ability to carry throughout our neighborhood. I would hear her as she was calling to get her daughter's attention. It didn't matter if Elle wasn't that far from her—she would yell out her name just the same. I think she found joy in calling her daughter's name, like it was music to her ears. It was clear to me that she found joy in being a mother.

I met Deanna shortly after she moved into my complex. My boys were outside, playing, and she was outside with Elle, talking to them. When I went looking for them, she ran right over and introduced herself with a big friendly smile and a warm handshake. It took me only minutes to realize that I liked this person and wanted to get to know her. Deanna went out of her way to compliment others and make sure that when you walked away from talking with her, you had a big smile on your face. That's how I always felt around her, happy and inspired. Her personality was infectious; she was so animated when she would talk. Even the simplest story told by her seemed less ordinary than when told by someone else.

Many times I would come home after the kids got out of school and see Deanna and Elle playing outside together. Whether she was trying to make a volcano with baking soda and vinegar in her front yard or drawing pictures with chalk on the street, Deanna was the kind of mother who played just as hard as the kids in the neighborhood. She was always full of fun ideas. The kids would get so riled up playing with her. I have never seen a woman throw a football like she did. I was secretly envious of that. If we were going to the park, she made sure we stopped to buy cupcakes. If we were swimming in the pool, she would have a handful of marbles she would throw and have the kids dive for. If we were going to have dinner, she would make sure the waiter gave each child a balloon to play with. Nobody in the neighborhood could walk by her without her stopping them to say hello and chat.

As much as Deanna liked to have fun, when the sun started to go down, she would say to Elle, "Time to go inside, eat dinner, and take a shower." We had many conversations about raising children, always worrying whether we were doing enough, trying to figure out ways to do more. Many mornings, when I would come home from work, I would see Deanna outside with a big smile on her face, seeing Elle off to school. It always put a smile on my face.

I admired Deanna so much as a mother. She reminded me to stop what I was doing and play with my kids—to have fun and not take myself too seriously—and that making someone smile is a great gift.

I am forever changed by knowing such a wonderful woman.

Elle and Deanna

Remembered

Of the thousands of employees I've known, I can tell you that Deanna was truly one of a kind. I've used many words to describe her. *Genuine, dynamic, sincere, honest,* and *open* are just a few. Her presence could never go unnoticed. When she walked into a room, all eyes turned toward her. She had a grace and glow about her that was unmistakable. . . . My wife, Nancy, likened Deanna to a thoroughbred racehorse—beautiful, strong, feisty, and always determined to get to the finish line first. She always made you feel like you were special. Her energy and enthusiasm were contagious. She never forgot your name and even knew your family's and your birthday.

—Deanna's employer, Robert Denberg,
owner of Restoration Dry Cleaning Network

I want you to know that Deanna was one of my all-time favorite cousins and one of my all-time favorite human beings. Always smiling. Always positive and encouraging.

—Cousin Ben

Like the stars in the sky, full of smiles and endless energy, Deanna would light up a room.

—Marcia

I will always remember Deanna as my super fun, warm, and welcoming cousin, who made me feel right at home whenever I was in Florida. She had a fabulous gift of always making me feel so special.

—Cousin Cambria

Ten months after Deanna passed away, Cambria and Logan's first child, a daughter, was born on Deanna's birthday.

Energy, enthusiasm, and passion for life—she always had a way of inspiring those around her to be the best they could be.

—Logan

I knew your daughter. She was trying to cope with bulimia. She was very sweet. I liked her a lot.

—My physician, Dr. Shimazu

(I was literally dumbfounded as he had only met Deanna on one occasion, for maybe an hour at the most, sixteen years before, yet he remembered her and the reason for her visit.)

I remember contemplating how I could best resemble Deanna's zeal for life. She spoke no words of malice. I will miss my cousin. From death, there is life as seen in Elle, and hopefully, she will grow up to have Deanna's quality traits.

—Cousin Sawyer

Deanna was a great person, and I will never forget her. She was outgoing, friendly, and cared about other people.

—Cousin Christian

She was beautiful, like a fashion model, and so kind. We admired her love for animals and her work with Guide Dogs for the Blind. She was a compassionate and caring individual, now at peace and free from the pain that was tormenting her inside. We will never forget wonderful Deanna.

—Carol

What a special woman Deanna was—such a big heart and caring soul.

—Sharon

Thank you, Deanna, for being a wonderful friend and mentor to me during a very hard time in my life. I will always remember your smile and love for others.

—Tracy

The world has lost a beautiful person. Her extraordinary kindness will be remembered by all who knew her.

—A friend

We will always remember what a loving and doting mother she was to Elmo and her vivacious personality. We will all truly miss her.

—Cousins Michael and Lisa

Deanna was such a force. So full of life. So zany. That's why everyone loved her.

—Patti

I remember my fortieth birthday, and thank you, Deanna, for being such a part of my special day. You were a ball of fire with so much love and happiness to give the world. Elle was also there, having a ball and so happy. I am thankful to have had you as part of my life, and you will be in my heart forever. I love you and thank you for making me smile.

—Michal

Is There a
Message Here?

Life can't always be understood.

Music was one of Deanna's passions; from classical to rock, she loved all of it. She could identify most singers and musicians from hearing just a snippet of their work. She played the piano and the guitar. Her dancing was full of energy, passion, and gusto.

On what would have been Deanna's thirty-seventh birthday, February 11, 2012, Whitney Houston, one of America's best-selling female vocal artists of all time, passed away. She and Deanna had the same demons—alcohol and prescription drugs—and they contributed to the death of both of them.

Another musical coincidence the same year was the death of Amy Winehouse. She was an English singer and songwriter known for her powerful deep contralto vocals and her eclectic mix of musical genres. She was extremely popular and died of alcohol poisoning about five months after Deanna.

Deanna knew she had a problem but kept trying to handle it. She fought continuously to overcome addiction. I feel the words from "I'm Coming Home" by J. Cole and Skylar Grey, one of her favorite songs, are appropriate:

I'm coming home, I'm coming home.
Tell the world I'm coming home.
Let the rain wash away all the pain of yesterday!
I know my kingdom awaits,
And they've forgiven my mistakes.

I'm coming home, I'm coming home.

It's not just celebrities. Multitudes of people are afflicted with addictive personalities. They find it extremely difficult, if not impossible, to cure themselves, to break their dependencies. Scores of people lose their jobs, friends, family—literally everything. Their lives! I wish it were as simple as just saying no! Deanna struggled daily. She went several times to classes, meetings, doctors, even hospitals. As hard as she tried to abstain, and she was successful for short periods, her compulsions recurred, prompting one relapse after another.

I hope someday medical research will pave the way to a greater understanding of the brain and how these people can be saved.

The First Anniversary

I Hear You

Deanna spoke to me on the first anniversary of her death, and then she spoke again on the second anniversary of her death. Now I have an expectation that this will continue. I fervently hope that it will.

Laine and I wanted to spend the day by ourselves, participating in an activity that Deanna would have enjoyed doing, an activity where we could reminisce all day. We decided to hike through the mountains above Crystal Cove, where we could see the ocean toward the completion of the trail. The trail was pretty rugged and steep in several places. I had been on it a few times before so knew a little of what to expect, but it was new to Laine. However, this time was different. First, a few mountain bikers came whizzing by. I immediately thought of Steve, Deanna's boyfriend, and wondered if Deanna was trying to tell me to keep in touch with him, to help him cope. Then a few hours later, we got our first glimpse of the ocean, with several dolphins swimming by. They looked like they were having a wonderful and happy time. The only other instance that I had ever seen dolphins in the wild was when Deanna and I were on a ferry boat going from Australia to Kangaroo Island. The dolphins were only about three feet from the prow of the ship, looking at us, actually appearing to smile. It seemed as though they were protecting and guiding the ship as it motored across the rough waters of the Southern Pacific Ocean. We watched them the entire time. And what a happy time. Seeing them again, I felt that Deanna is every bit as free and happy as she was that day in Australia.

Laine and I finished our day having dinner at Crystal Cove in a restaurant right on the beach. Deanna had a good friend whose family used to invite her to go swimming at Crystal Cove, where they owned a small beach house. Now, the state has taken it over, and Crystal Cove is a state park where people can rent the original, remodeled beach houses. It was the perfect place for us to be on that day.

The Second
Anniversary

As we did the year before, Laine and I spent the entire day making it a Deanna Day. We rented bikes and rode all the way down to the end of Newport Beach Peninsula and down Pacific Coast Highway, almost to Huntington Beach. Both of us were a little sore, but we knew Deanna would be proud of our effort.

We returned the bikes, and to our surprise, just a few doors away, there was a tattoo parlor. Deanna had tattoos, and she knew I really did not like them. But I decided we should go in and get some information and not be reluctant to understand the art of tattoo. We walked through the door, and inside sat three heavily tattooed young men. At first, it was maybe a little intimidating, but it turned out that all of them were very nice. We learned an abundance of valuable information, and I left thinking maybe I should get a tattoo in honor of Deanna, perhaps a little dolphin about an inch high, like the one she got at nineteen as a freshman at Northern Arizona University. I thought Deanna would be proud.

Next stop, Starbucks, one of Deanna's all-time favorite places. We made a point of going to the one she frequented when in California. A lady, probably in her late thirties or early forties, walked in. She had tattoos literally from head to toe. That's pretty unusual for Newport Beach. We talked with her at length, trying to figure out her reasons for so many tattoos. It seemed that we were inundated with tattoos that day. Was Deanna telling us to get a tattoo?

Laine and I discussed the possibility at dinner. My major concern was Elle. I didn't want my granddaughter to have a tattoo and was concerned she might want one especially since her mother had one. So I thought I'd clear it with her father first.

Coincidently, that very day, Elle had asked her dad about tattoos after seeing an advertisement in a magazine. He told her what he told me, that Deanna had said she wished she could get rid of her tattoos but was afraid of the scarring and the pain. And she was adamant that Elle never get one. She didn't even like to see Elle put on one of those temporary ones that children enjoy. Then Joe reminded me that at my age, it wouldn't be all that long until a dolphin would look like an eel.

Steve also had a tattoo moment that day. He'd been thinking that I might encourage him to get a tattoo in honor of Deanna.

It certainly seemed that Deanna's tattoo messages to everyone close to her were loud and clear on the second anniversary!

The Third Anniversary

This anniversary took me to Flagstaff, Arizona, a beautiful mountain town. There I renewed my friendship with Connie, Deanna's stepmother during her early teen years, and had the opportunity to meet her husband, Ed, and visit Northern Arizona University, where Deanna was a student her freshman year of college.

Connie is a very intuitive and insightful person, and Ed was a longtime news director for KNX, now retired. Together, they had helped me with the editing of this book. Their help was invaluable and greatly appreciated.

One of Deanna's favorite classes at NAU gave her the opportunity to work in a battered-women's shelter where most of the women were Indians. She relished her experience there, put in many extra hours, and learned about the Indian culture in the United States.

Another accomplishment Deanna was very proud of was that she made the soccer team and became their goalie. Unfortunately, an ankle injury prevented her from completing the year. Although she was very disappointed, she directed her attention to other activities.

I truly wanted to see the NAU campus and was lucky that Sawyer, my nephew, was able to give me a guided tour. Although I still recognized much of the campus, there were many new and interesting buildings. Lots of the students were on bikes, dressed similarly to the way they were when Deanna was a student. The San Francisco Peaks surrounding the school were beautiful. Lots of snowcapped mountaintops were readily visible along with unparalleled natural scenery. Sawyer is Deanna's second cousin to attend NAU; Jordon was the first. So officially, Sawyer is the third lumberjack of the family.

Although the drive from Newport to Flagstaff is fairly long, it gave me the wonderful opportunity to relive some of Deanna's s life there. I especially enjoyed all the teasing she tolerated regarding the humungous statue of Louie the Lumberjack and all the singing of "Louie, Louie" by Laine and myself.

Again, many memories were rekindled and indulged in on the third anniversary.

The final verse of a poem by Ellen Brenneman

And think of her as living
In the hearts of those she touched . . .
For nothing loved is ever lost—
And she was loved so much.

CPSIA information can be obtained at www.ICGtesting.com
Printed in the USA
BVOW07s1948040215

386419BV00001B/4/P